THE UNIVERSE

# Jupiter

Tim Goss

**H** www.heinemann.co.uk/library
Visit our website to find out more information about Heinemann Library books.

To order:
☎ Phone 44 (0) 1865 888066
▤ Send a fax to 44 (0) 1865 314091
▢ Visit the Heinemann Bookshop at www.heinemann.co.uk/library to browse our catalogue and order online.

First published in Great Britain by Heinemann, Halley Court, Jordan Hill, Oxford, OX2 8EJ, part of Harcourt Education.
Raintree is a registered trademark of Harcourt Education Ltd.

Editorial: Nick Hunter and Rachel Howells
Design: Richard Parker and Tinstar Design
Illustrations: Art Construction
Picture Research: Mica Brancic
Production: Julie Carter

Originated by Modern Age
Printed and bound in China by Leo Paper Group

ISBN 9780431154732
11 10 09 08 07
10 9 8 7 6 5 4 3 2 1

**British Library Cataloguing in Publication Data**
Goss, Tim
Jupiter. - (The universe)
523.4'5

A full catalogue record for this book is available from the British Library.

**Acknowledgements**
The Publishers would like to thank the following for permission to reproduce photographs: pp. 4, 9, 12, 15, 18, 20, 25, 28 NASA/JPL/Caltech; pp. 5, 26, 27 NASA; p. 6 D. Van Ravenswaay/Photo Researchers, Inc.; pp. 7, 8, 13, 21, 29 NASA/JPL/University of Arizona; p. 10 NASA/JPL/Cornell University; p. 11 Bettman/Corbis; pp. 14, 16 NASA/JPL/DLR (German Aerospace Center); p. 17 NASA/JPL/U.S. Geological Survey; P. 19 European Southern Observatory (ESO); p. 22 NASA/JPL/California Institute of Technology; p. 23 NASA/ESA, John Clarke/University of Michigan, NASA and the Hubble Heritage Team (STScl/AURA); p. 24 Courtesy of Calvin J. Hamilton/www.solarviews.com

Cover photograph reproduced with permission of NASA/JPL/Space Science Institute.

The publishers would like to thank Geza Gyuk of the Adler Planetarium, Chicago, for his assistance in the preparation of this book.

Every effort has been made to contact copyright holders of any material reproduced in this book. Any omissions will be rectified in subsequent printings if notice is given to the publishers.

# Contents

Any words appearing in the text in bold, **like this**, are explained in the glossary.

# Where in the sky is Jupiter?

Jupiter is the fifth planet from the Sun in our **solar system**. It is also the second brightest planet. Venus is the only planet that is brighter. Jupiter is so bright that when it appears in the night sky, you can see it without a **telescope**. It looks like a silver star.

## King of the planets

Jupiter is the largest planet in our solar system. Its diameter, the distance right through the middle of the planet from one side to the other, is 11 times as large as Earth's. That means you could put 11 Earths side by side inside Jupiter. If you stuffed as many Earths as possible inside of Jupiter, around 1,000 Earths would fit.

The mark for which the planet Jupiter is best known is the large spot that you see about halfway down on the striped planet.

## The king's colours

If you view Jupiter through a telescope, you can see that it has alternating stripes of cream and brown. The cream stripes are called **zones**. The brown stripes are called **belts**. Different **chemicals** in each layer make the different colours. Most of Jupiter is made up of clouds and gas layers. It is one of the planets called the Gas Giants. The other Gas Giants are Saturn, Uranus, and Neptune.

When an image of Jupiter is placed with images of the other planets, its larger size is easy to recognize. Jupiter is the fifth planet from the Sun (Earth is third).

## The solar system

A solar system is a group of objects in space that move in **orbits** around a central star. The objects can be planets, moons, **comets**, meteors, and **asteroids**. The Sun is the central star in our solar system. **Gravity** from the Sun pulls on all of the objects in our solar system. This keeps Jupiter and the other objects in our solar system from flying off into space.

Jupiter can be seen from Earth without a **telescope** even though it is usually about 772 million kilometres (480 million miles) away.

## How long is a Jupiter year?

One year is the time it takes for a planet to make one circle (**revolution**) around the Sun. On Earth, a year is 365 days long. It takes Jupiter almost 12 Earth years to make a single revolution. As it **orbits** the Sun, Jupiter travels at about 47,000 kilometres (29,000 miles) per hour. Earth orbits the Sun at a faster speed of about 107,000 kilometres (66,600 miles) per hour. When you combine Jupiter's slower orbital speed with its greater distance from the Sun, you can understand why Jupiter's year is so long.

The difference in the revolutions of Earth and Jupiter is what causes Jupiter's different positions in the sky when you look at it from Earth. Earth keeps passing Jupiter, as the planets orbit the Sun, because Earth's revolution is much faster than

These photos show nine stages of Jupiter's rotation. Jupiter's rotation is almost two and a half times faster than Earth's.

Jupiter's. As Earth is about to catch up to and pass Jupiter, Jupiter appears to be in front of Earth. After Earth passes Jupiter, Jupiter appears to be behind Earth.

## Jupiter days are very short

A **day** is the time it takes for a planet to spin around once on its **axis**: the imaginary line that runs from a planet's north pole to its south pole. One Earth day is 24 hours long. A day on Jupiter lasts a little less than 10 hours. Jupiter spins faster on its axis than any other planet.

## How did Jupiter get its name?

**Astronomers** named Jupiter after the king of the Roman gods. This god was the ruler of everything in the sky. He was believed to be the god who brought light to the world. Paintings of the god Jupiter often show him with a lightning bolt in his hand.

# What's special about Jupiter?

Everything weighs more on Jupiter. The **gravity** on Jupiter is much stronger than on Earth. It is about two and a half times stronger. If you weigh 36 kilograms (80 pounds) on Earth, you would weigh 90 kilograms (200 pounds) on Jupiter. That's because the force holding you to the **surface** of the planet is pulling you down much harder.

## Jupiter makes its own heat

On Earth, the Sun provides nearly all of the warmth that we feel. The Sun's heat energy warms the ground and the oceans. Earth cannot give off any more energy than it receives. Jupiter, however, gives off more heat than it gets from the Sun. How does this happen?

The image on the left shows the true colour of Jupiter. Colour filters were used in the image on the right to help scientists study the planet. The darkest blue areas are called hot spots.

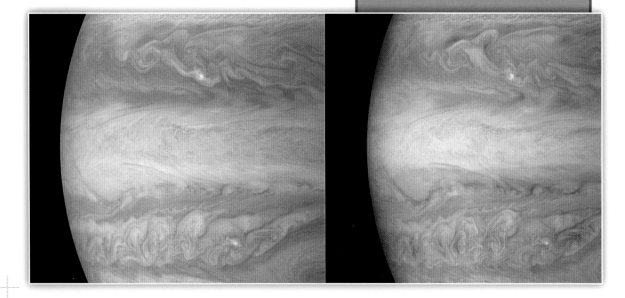

Jupiter's **core** is in the very centre of the planet. The temperature there is many thousands of degrees, maybe even as high as 33,000°C (60,000°F), and it used to be hotter! Heat energy from the core rises to the surface. Where did this heat come from and why has it not run out? When each planet first formed from bits of dust, rocks, and ice, a lot of heat was created when gravity squeezed these objects together. The heat from the planets' formation has been escaping slowly over millions of years. Small planets, such as Earth, lose their heat quickly. Large planets, such as Jupiter, have much more heat to begin with and lose it very slowly.

This image gives a close-up look at Jupiter's ring system.

## Jupiter has rings

Jupiter has a narrow set of **rings** that you can see with a **telescope**. Information from the *Pioneer 10* and *11* missions in 1973 and 1974 led scientists to think there might be rings around Jupiter. No one saw the rings until the *Voyager I* mission sent back images in 1979. The planet Saturn also has rings, but Jupiter's rings are smaller and darker. Jupiter's rings seem to be made of dust and rock particles.

## Jupiter is a giant magnet

Jupiter is one of six planets that have **magnetic fields** bigger than the planets themselves. The other planets are Earth, Mercury, Saturn, Uranus, and Neptune. A magnetic field cannot be seen. It fills the areas around a magnet. Inside a magnetic field, the motion of electric charges and other magnets are affected.

The magnetic field around Jupiter is huge. It stretches away from the planet at least 6.4 million kilometres (4 million miles) in every direction. That is bigger than the Sun!

Particles flowing out from the Sun, called the solar wind, sweep Jupiter's magnetic field into a long "tail". Jupiter's magnetic tail stretches more than 966 million kilometres (600 million miles). It goes beyond the **orbit** of Saturn!

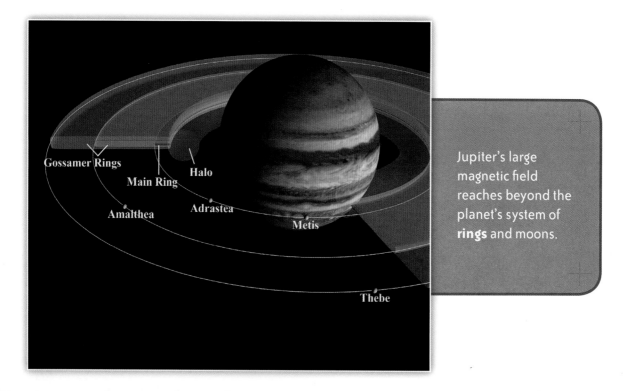

Gossamer Rings

Halo

Main Ring

Amalthea

Adrastea

Metis

Thebe

Jupiter's large magnetic field reaches beyond the planet's system of **rings** and moons.

# Does Jupiter have moons?

On 6 January 1610, an **astronomer** called Galileo Galilei saw what appeared to be three stars lined up with Jupiter. When he looked the next night, the positions of the stars had changed. The positions continued to change every night. Galileo realized that the objects he was looking at were **moons**. They were orbiting Jupiter just like Earth's Moon goes around Earth. Later, Galileo saw that there were actually four moons orbiting Jupiter.

Galileo's discovery of Jupiter's moons was one of the most important discoveries ever made. The old ideas about the universe were that the Earth stayed still and everything else moved around it. But the moons Galileo discovered moved around Jupiter, not around Earth. His discovery supported the ideas of scientists Nicolaus Copernicus and Johannes Kepler. They thought Earth and the other planets moved around the Sun.

The Italian astronomer Galileo was born in 1564 and died in 1642. During his lifetime, he made many important discoveries.

## Astronomers have found many moons

Beyond the Galilean **moons** are a swarm of many more moons – 55 at the last count! All of these are very small. The furthest known moon is so small and new that it doesn't even have a name! It is more than 24 million kilometres (17 million miles) from Jupiter and takes almost 1,000 days to **orbit** once!

Jupiter's four closest moons are much closer to Jupiter than Earth's Moon is to Earth. This is an artist's impression of what Jupiter and its closest moons would look like from near the moon Callisto (lower right). The other three moons, top to bottom, are Io, Europa, and Ganymede.

More small moons are still being discovered around Jupiter. The final total is still not known, but could be as high as 100 moons!

## The Galilean moon Io

Io is about the size of Earth's Moon. Io is mostly flat, but there are mountains on it that are about 10 kilometres (almost 6 miles) high. In 1979, *Voyager 1* discovered active **volcanoes** on Io. As far as scientists know, only Earth and Io have active volcanoes. Io's volcanoes are more active and hotter than Earth's. The *Voyager* missions discovered more than 16 volcanoes erupting on Io.

Most of Io's **craters** were caused by volcanic actions. The largest volcano on Io, called Pele, throws out material into an area the size of the country of Italy. Io's **surface** is spotted with red, yellow, white, and orange-black. The colours are from the **sulphur** in Io's top layer, the **crust**.

Io has more active volcanoes than any other object in the **solar system**.

## The Galilean moon Europa

Europa is almost as big as Earth's **Moon**. There are very few **craters** on Europa. It is the smoothest object in the **solar system**. Because there are not very many craters, scientists think that the **surface** of Europa is very young compared to that of the other moons. The surface might only be a few million years old. Europa's icy surface reflects a lot of sunlight. It reflects about five times more light than Earth's Moon reflects.

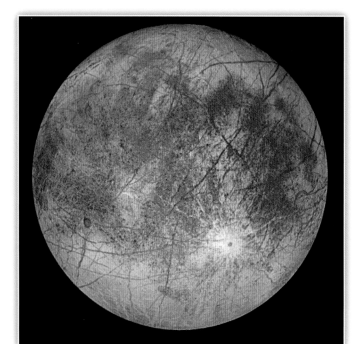

The **crust** of Europa is made of ice and is probably about 100 kilometres (60 miles) thick, though no one knows for certain. Some large areas on Europa have lots of icebergs. Below Europa's surface, temperatures may be warm enough for an ocean of water.

Images of Europa show thousands of cracks and ridges criss-crossing one another over and over again. Some of these cracks are thousands of kilometres long.

## The Galilean moon Ganymede

Ganymede is the largest moon in our solar system. It is more than one and a half times bigger than Earth's Moon. It is also bigger than the planet Mercury. Part of Ganymede's surface is covered by dark areas with lots of craters. The rest is lighter and has grooves, which are long lines that cut into the moon's surface. Some grooves are thousands of kilometres long. The dark areas are very old and the light areas are much younger.

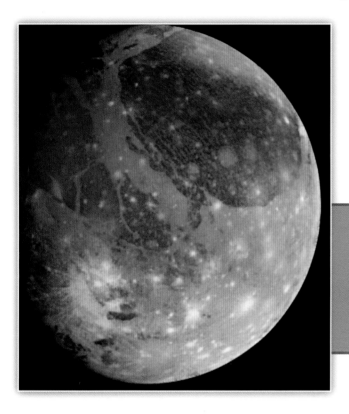

Ganymede has its own **magnetic field**. This makes scientists think that it has metals in its **core**.

## The Galilean moon Callisto

Callisto is the Galilean moon furthest from Jupiter. It is the third largest moon in our solar system. Only Ganymede and Saturn's moon Titan are bigger. Callisto's surface is covered with cracked ice and craters. Some of the craters are very large. Callisto has more craters than any other object in our solar system.

The *Galileo* spacecraft discovered that, like the moon Europa, Callisto might have an ocean under its icy **crust**. Scientists have also learned from the *Galileo* that **oxygen** may be inside the ice and rocks on Callisto.

Callisto's **craters** are called impact craters. They formed when **meteorites**, **comets**, and **asteroids** crashed into its **surface**. Callisto's many craters have made scientists think that the **moon's** surface is very old. In fact, they think Callisto's surface has not been remade for billions of years. If **molten** rock or ice had covered the surface since then, most of the craters would have been wiped away. Only a very old surface would have had time to collide with so many objects.

# How's the weather on Jupiter?

Since Jupiter is so far away from the Sun, it is always cold. At the top of Jupiter's cloud layer, the temperatures get as cold as –150°C (–235°F). It is also very windy. The fastest winds, near the planet's **equator**, can reach speeds of up to 550 kilometres (340 miles ) per hour. There are also thunderstorms.

## Cloudy

Jupiter's **atmosphere** is made up of mostly **hydrogen** and **helium**. There are three cloud layers within the atmosphere, which are about 50 kilometres (30 miles) thick from top to bottom. The top layer of clouds is made of **ammonia** ice. The middle layer has crystals made of a combination of ammonia, hydrogen, and **sulphur**. The bottom layer contains water ice and possibly even liquid water.

The **chemicals** in Jupiter's cloud layers react with the tiny bit of **carbon** in the planet's atmosphere. This creates new chemical **compounds** in different colours. These are the reds, browns, and blues we see in Jupiter's clouds.

Some areas of the clouds look dark and others appear lighter. The dark areas are called **belts** and the light areas are called **zones**. These form the coloured bands we see around the planet. Belts and zones are found in different places at different times. They also change size.

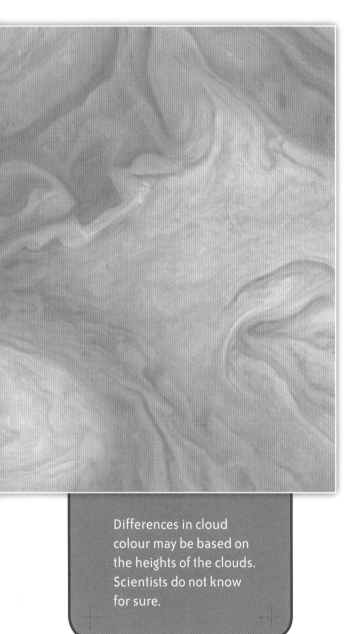

Differences in cloud colour may be based on the heights of the clouds. Scientists do not know for sure.

## Windy

Winds on Jupiter are formed in a different way from those on Earth. The winds on Earth are caused by differences in temperatures. Hot air rises and cold air sinks. The greater the difference in temperature, the stronger the wind when the two air masses run into each other. The Sun warms Earth's **atmosphere**. It is often about 38°C (100°F) warmer at the **equator** than at the North or South Pole.

On Jupiter, the temperatures at the north and south poles and the equator are almost the same. Because it is so far away, the Sun does not have as much effect on Jupiter as it does on Earth. Scientists know that Jupiter's atmosphere, which is below the planet's clouds, is very windy. Heat from Jupiter's **core** flows out into the atmosphere and warms the clouds. This probably creates the wind currents.

A picture of Jupiter taken using infrared light. Different temperatures are shown as different colours. The bright spot on the left is Jupiter's moon Io.

## Storms and spots

The storms inside Jupiter's **belts** and **zones** have lasted for many years. One storm called the Great Red Spot has lasted for at least 300 years. The Great Red Spot is an area of dark red and brown clouds that spin in a circle. The clouds complete one circle every six days. The winds blow at about 400 kilometres (250 miles) per hour. The Great Red Spot covers an area bigger than two Earths. It is the most powerful storm in the **solar system**.

## The white storm

The *Galileo* space mission returned images of two white storm centres combining into one big storm. This huge storm had an oval shape, like an egg, and it is still active. The only storm bigger than this one is the Great Red Spot.

This image shows a close-up of the Great Red Spot.

# What would I need if I went to Jupiter?

To visit Jupiter, you would need a lot of equipment to survive. You would need tanks of air so you could breathe. The **atmosphere** below the clouds is a poisonous mixture of **hydrogen** and **helium** gases, with tiny amounts of **ammonia** and **methane**. Since Jupiter is a Gas Giant, there is no solid ground to land on. You would need a spacecraft that could fly. As you dropped further down towards the **core**, the hydrogen and helium gases would slowly change into a liquid form. Your spacecraft would also have to be a submarine!

## A deep sea

If you swim to a great depth in an ocean on Earth, your ears will "pop" from the **pressure** of the water. The same thing would happen on Jupiter as you moved from the clouds to deep inside the planet.

Colour filters make the planet's belts, zones, and Great Red Spot really stand out.

The *Galileo* spacecraft discovered that, like the moon Europa, Callisto might have an ocean under its icy **crust**. Scientists have also learned from the *Galileo* that **oxygen** may be inside the ice and rocks on Callisto.

The weight of all the many thousands of kilometres of **atmosphere** and liquid **hydrogen** and **helium** would crush you. Only high in the atmosphere, where the clouds are, is the **pressure** similar to the pressure of the air we breathe on Earth.

By the time you went about 21,000 kilometres (13,000 miles) down into Jupiter's sea, the pressure would be more than 3 million times what it is on Earth's **surface**. That is enough to make the liquid hydrogen turn into metal. No one knows much about liquid metallic hydrogen because it cannot exist on Earth. This sea of metallic hydrogen is about 40,000 kilometres (25,000 miles) deep.

## A super light show on Jupiter

If you had visited Jupiter in July 1994, you would have seen a **comet** crash into the planet. Scientists first saw the comet in March 1993. As they studied it, they learned that in early July 1992, the comet had come close enough to Jupiter to break into 21 pieces. Some of these pieces were more than 2 kilometres (1 mile) wide. Scientists were able to predict when pieces of the comet would crash into Jupiter.

In July 1994, the pieces plunged into Jupiter's atmosphere and exploded from the impact. The explosions were so bright that **astronomers** on Earth could see the light reflected from Jupiter's **moons**. The *Galileo* spacecraft took pictures of the collisions.

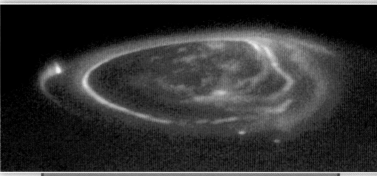

An **aurora** is a reaction between particles in the magnetic field of a planet and gases in the planet's atmosphere. Jupiter's **auroras** create a light show of electric blue.

## What makes the magnetic field magnetic?

The high pressure in the sea of liquid metallic hydrogen squeezes the hydrogen **molecules** so tightly that they break apart. It is like trying to stuff a lot of grapes into a box. If you pack them too tightly, the grapes will burst. When hydrogen becomes metallic, electricity flows through it much more easily. Scientists think the electric currents in the liquid metallic hydrogen create Jupiter's **magnetic field**.

# What is inside Jupiter?

Looking at the inside of Jupiter, one of the Gas Giants, is different from looking at the inside of one of the Rocky Planets, such as Earth. Below the **atmosphere** on Earth is the solid **surface** of the planet. The **crust** is below the surface. Under the crust is the **mantle**, which is almost completely solid. Finally, there is the **core**, which has both solid parts and **molten** parts. Jupiter is different because it has no surface or crust.

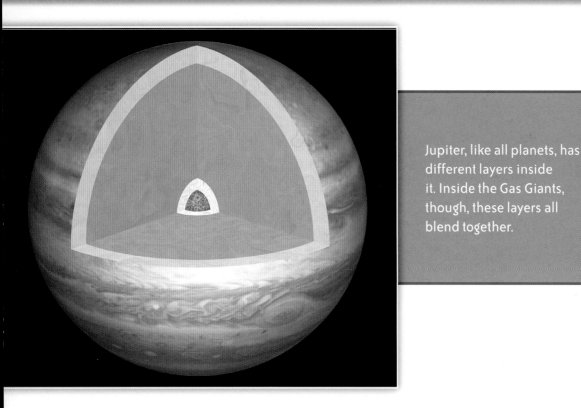

Jupiter, like all planets, has different layers inside it. Inside the Gas Giants, though, these layers all blend together.

Jupiter's atmosphere of **hydrogen** and **helium** simply gets thicker and denser the further towards the centre you go. The region of liquid metallic hydrogen can be thought of as an inner mantle.

## Jupiter's core

Jupiter does have a huge core, and it might be solid. Scientists think the core is made of rock and metal, but no one knows for sure. Jupiter's core is about the size of two Earths. The temperature of the core is about 17,000°C (30,000°F). The slow escape of this heat affects the winds on Jupiter. Some of the heat gets through holes in the clouds, creating areas called hot spots.

## We don't know much about what's inside Jupiter

Scientists cannot measure the inside of Jupiter directly. The hot temperatures would melt any **probe** that tried to go into the interior of the planet. The high **pressures** would also crush scientific instruments. A probe dropped by the *Galileo* spacecraft lasted less than an hour.

The *Galileo* probe's heat shield and parachute helped it enter Jupiter's atmosphere.

# Could I ever go to Jupiter?

To visit Jupiter, you would need a lot of special equipment to survive the long journey. You would need tanks of **oxygen** so you could breathe, and specially-designed spacecraft that could both fly and hold up under very strong **pressure**.

From the water ice on Jupiter's **moons**, you could get drinking water, oxygen, and **hydrogen** fuel. However, none of this would help you survive the high levels of **radiation** around Jupiter. You would not last more than a couple of minutes without a heavy-duty spacecraft. Jupiter's strong **magnetic field** holds the radiation close to the planet.

The *Space Shuttle Discovery* took the Hubble Space **Telescope** into space. Much of the information that scientists have about the planets comes from this telescope.

## You can "visit" with a space probe

**Space probes** have provided much of the information that we have about Jupiter. There have been five Jupiter missions. The *Pioneer 10* and *11* missions took the first photos of Jupiter and its moons in 1973 and 1974. We also learned more about the magnetic field and the high levels of radiation. *Pioneer 11* discovered Jupiter's **ring** system. In 1979, the *Voyager 1* and *2* space probes showed us details of Jupiter's clouds, moons, and ring system as they flew by Jupiter on their way to study Saturn, Uranus, and Neptune.

In this photo, scientists are fitting together the *Galileo* space probe. They have to wear special clothes and work in a room designed to keep dust away from the delicate instruments of the space probe.

## The Galileo probe

The National Aeronautics and Space Administration (NASA) and the European Space Agency (ESA) launched the *Galileo* space probe on 18 October 1989. The *Galileo* probe had two parts. One part was sent into the **atmosphere** of Jupiter to collect information about what **chemicals** it is made of. It worked for 57 minutes before falling so deep that the high pressure and temperature destroyed it. The second part, the **orbiter**, stayed in space circling Jupiter and sending back information. It took many pictures and other data. It was finally destroyed in September 2003.

# Fact File

|  | JUPITER | EARTH |
| --- | --- | --- |
| Average distance from the Sun | 778 million kilometres (484 million miles) | 150 million kilometres (93 million miles) |
| Revolution around the Sun | 11.9 Earth years | 1 Earth year (365 days) |
| Average speed of orbit | 13 kilometres/second (8.1 miles/second) | 30 kilometres/second (18.6 miles/second) |
| Diameter at equator | 142,984 kilometres (88,846 miles) | 12,756 kilometres (7,926 miles) |
| Time for one rotation | 9 hours, 50 minutes | 24 hours |
| Atmosphere | **hydrogen** and **helium** | nitrogen, **oxygen** |
| Moons and rings | at least 63 moons and 3 rings | 1 moon and no rings |
| Temperature range | (**atmosphere** to **core**) –150°C (–235°F) to 17,000°C (30,000°F) | (**surface** only) –69°C (–92°F) to 58°C (136°F) |

Colour filters were used to make this partial view of Jupiter more dramatic.

## A trip to Jupiter from Earth

- When Jupiter and Earth come closest to each other in their **orbits**, they are 591 million kilometres (367 million miles) apart.

- Travelling to Jupiter by car at 113 kilometres (70 miles) per hour would take at least 600 years.

- Travelling to Jupiter by rocket at 11 kilometres (7 miles) per second would take at least 607 days.

Jupiter is shown here with Io, the planet's closest moon, to its left.

## More interesting facts

- Jupiter spins around on its **axis** about 27 times faster than Earth does. Jupiter is shaped like a slightly flattened ball because it spins so quickly.

- Jupiter has a very tiny **moon** called Leda. It is only about 16 kilometres (10 miles) wide. This means that it is more than 200 times smaller than Earth's Moon.

- Metis is Jupiter's fastest-moving moon.

# Glossary

**ammonia** strong-smelling gas found in Jupiter's atmosphere

**asteroid** large piece of floating rock left over from when the planets formed

**astronomer** person who studies objects in outer space

**atmosphere** all of the gases that surround an object in outer space

**aurora** colourful display caused by charged particles in an atmosphere

**axis** imaginary line through the middle of an object in space, around which it spins as it rotates

**belt** dark layer of clouds wrapped around Jupiter that alternates with zones

**carbon** element found in all plants and animals

**chemical** form of matter, or substance

**comet** ball of ice and rock that orbits the Sun

**compound** combination of two or more elements

**core** centre of a planet

**crater** bowl-shaped hole in the ground that is made by a meteorite or a burst of lava

**crust** top, solid layer of an object in outer space. The outer part of the crust is called the surface.

**day** time it takes for a planet to spin around its axis once

**equator** imaginary line around the middle of a planet

**gravity** invisible force that pulls an object towards the centre of another object in outer space

**helium** gas found on many planets. It is used on Earth to make balloons float in the air.

**hydrogen** substance found on many planets. On Earth, hydrogen gas mixes with oxygen gas to form water.

**magnetic field** region in which the motion of electrical particles and magnets is affected

**mantle** middle layer of a planet or moon. It lies between the core and the crust.

**meteorite** piece of rock or dust that lands on the surface of a planet or moon from space

**methane** chemical found in gas form in many atmospheres

**molecule** tiny unit made up of two or more atoms of a substance joined together

**molten** melted by heat into a liquid form

**moon** object that floats in an orbit around a planet

**orbit** curved path of one object in space moving around another object

**orbiter** spacecraft that flies in orbit around a planet

**oxygen** gas found in the atmospheres of some planets; used by mammals to breathe

**pressure** force in the atmosphere or inner parts of a planet that presses in from all sides, due to the weight of all the material above and around

**probe** part of a space probe that leaves the orbiter and studies the atmosphere or surface of an object in space

**radiation** energy released in waves, particles, or rays. Heat and light are types of radiation.

**revolution** time it takes for a planet to travel once around the Sun (also known as a year)

**ring** circle-shaped group of dust and tiny rocks that travels in a close orbit around a planet

**solar system** group of objects in outer space that all float in orbits around a central star

**space probe** ship that carries computers and other instruments to study objects in outer space

**sulphur** yellow-coloured, powdery material. It is found on many planets in gas form.

**surface** part of a planet's crust layer that lies just below the planet's atmosphere

**telescope** instrument used by astronomers to study objects in outer space

**volcano** mountain built up from layers of hardened lava

**zone** light band of clouds wrapped around Jupiter that alternates with belts

# More books to read

*Atlas of Stars and Planets: A Beginner's Guide to the Universe*, Ian Ridpath (Philip's OS Publications, 2004)

*Stargazers' Guides: Can We Travel to the Stars?*, Rosalind Mist and Andrew Solway (Heinemann Library, 2006)

# Index